Ordinary

Ordinary

A poetic anthology of culture, immigration, & identity

Poems by
Laura Hyppolite

New Degree Press
Copyright © 2021 Laura Hyppolite
All rights reserved.

Ordinary
A poetic anthology of culture, immigration, & identity

ISBN	978-1-63676-868-7	*Paperback*
	978-1-63730-174-6	*Kindle Ebook*
	978-1-63730-312-2	*Ebook*

Contents

AUTHOR'S NOTE	13
PART 1. CULTURE	**19**
ONE OF MANY	20
POV	21
CORNROWS	22
CROWNED	24
REFLECTION	26
2 TRUTHS AND A LIE	29
MUTUAL HATE	31
GOLDEN FLOWER	32
BY THE VICTORS	34
THE ONES THEY CALL BOAT PEOPLE	35
NAME CALLING	37
DEPLETED	38
TASTES OF HAITI	39
SOUNDS OF HAITI	40
PAINT ME A PORTRAIT	41
PEARL OF THE ANTILLES	42
A PEOPLE OF NATURE	43
WHEN IT RAINS	44
A HOSPITABLE PEOPLE	45
COUNTRYSIDE	46
CITYSIDE	48
BLACKOUT	50
LOVE AND HATE	52
INTERGENERATIONAL	54

BLEMISH	56
HAITI CHERIE,	57
PART 2. IMMIGRATION	**59**
THE UNKNOWN	60
FINAL GOODBYE	61
A CONVERSATION BETWEEN A MOTHER AND A DAUGHTER	62
CLOUD NINE	63
BOARDING	65
ARRIVAL	66
BECOME A SPONGE	67
BECOME A SPONGE, PT. 2	69
IT	71
CALLING CARDS	73
OUR REASONS	75
INSIDE JOKE	76
MICROAGGRESSIONS	77
SCAPEGOAT	78
7.0	79
A GIRL WITH MANY HATS	80
SACRIFICES	81
FORWARD IN REVERSE	82
DREAM ON	83
MIRAGE	84
OUR OWN WORST ENEMY	85
AAVE	86
CRENGLISH	88
COPING	90
LOST MEMORIES	92
SILENT THREAT	94
SECRET'S OUT	95

CIRCLE OF MANIPULATION	97
FALSE HOPE	99
THE ODDS ARE NOT IN OUR FAVOR	100
ALLY	102
RECONCILIATION	104
OUR ULTIMATE DEMISE	106
PART 3. IDENTITY	**109**
REGRET	110
THE SUPER IMMIGRANTS	112
BITTER	113
TEAM EFFORT	114
UNSPOKEN	115
JUGGLING ACT	116
GOOD HAIR	117
REDEFINED	120
YOUR SMILE SAYS…	122
THE STORY HER EYES TOLD ME	124
THE STRANGER	127
LOVE LANGUAGE	129
IN A BUBBLE	131
A COMPLICATED LOVE STORY	133
A MIDNIGHT DRIVE-THRU KIND OF LOVE	134
TO THE REAL ONES	135
PASSBERBY	136
IN MY HEAD	137
FORESIGHT	139
AN ESCAPE	140
BETWEEN THE SOMETHINGS	142
INTROSPECTION	143
OREO	144
INTERSECTIONALITY	145

ABSPORTION   146
A WELCOMED OASIS   147
MIRROR ON THE WALL   148
ORDINARY   149
LESSONS LEARNED   151
LANDSCAPES   152
FINAL WORDS   153

ACKNOWLEDGEMENTS   155
APPENDIX   157

To Arguio and Chantal
The first dreamers

AUTHOR'S NOTE

To my readers,
(don't skip this part)

March 26, 2007. The day the story began. I disembarked the plane—a wide-eyed eight-year-old—expecting my life to change instantly. As I looked around the brightly lit John F. Kennedy Airport, I saw signs for restaurants I had never eaten at, advertisements for TV shows I never knew existed, and clothing with emblems I had never worn. The grandeur of the scene was overwhelming, but a woman's voice over the speakers interrupted the chaos brewing in my head. I caught a few words of what she was saying: "fly," "pass," and "tomorrow." When the monotonous voice of the announcement ended, I anticipated another voice to break through the static and offer the French or Creole translation. Wide-eyed, I waited. The voice never came. Looking back to those first moments on American soil, I find my naivety endearing, yet foolish. For many years, this blanket of ignorance veiled my view of the world. I missed the snide remarks, the suspicious gazes, the microaggressions. But I grew up. And I quickly recognized that the idealized world I was living in was nothing but a fabrication of my expectations. In the beginning, all I wanted to be was American—to embrace all parts of the culture while relinquishing the components of my own. Most of that stemmed from social pressure, but it was also a coping mechanism. To be American would also mean distancing myself from the negative connotations of being an immigrant, so it was easier to try to be *less* Haitian. I felt trapped and isolated in that mindset.

The Pew Research Center reports that there are over 44 million people in the United States who are classified as immigrants.[1] Some people think that when an immigrant comes to America, they come to comprehensively take in all aspects of what it means to American. This can be very damaging, especially to young immigrants who are conditioned to believe that to accept their new American culture, they would have to renounce the most genuine parts of themselves. Let me offer a different approach to this contested issue. *If one immigrates with the expectation of preserving themselves—perhaps even staying exactly who they were before—would the change in geography allow it?* This is where the waters get murky because I know that reality does not offer a direct answer to this question. It is far more complex. It was not enough for me to claim to be a Haitian that happens to live in America. There are many aspects of ourselves and our new world that are in contest, and sometimes we have to make a choice. Maybe it is this inner contest and a desire for transformation that yields an unruly desire for growth. I often wonder about the Haitian immigrants who are faced with making that choice. But there is the thing about Haitian people: we are resilient. We are no strangers to captivity, isolation, and rejection. We persevere beyond those confinements. We do not do it alone, though. Much of the growth we believe we have nurtured is instead embedded in our nature. And for that, we thank the motherland. Our ancestry has primed

---

1 Abby Budiman, "Key Findings about US Immigrants," *Pew Research Center*, August 20, 2020.

us for such growth to occur. From our ancestry, we build a profound connection with our true identity. A connection to that history is what made me want to be *more* Haitian. We learn from the mistakes of the past. We celebrate our accomplishments. And we draw on those moments to recount the narratives of the present. In "Ordinary," I intend to do just that: learn, celebrate, and tell stories.

At my roots, I am a storyteller. For years, most of the stories of my immigration experience have lived in my head, waiting to be told. Yet, while writing this book, I often struggled with feelings of imposter syndrome. *Who was I to be a voice for anyone but myself? What qualified my name to appear on this cover?* The more I asked myself this question, the more it became clear that I am not attempting to claim expertise in anything. I am recounting my experiences and my reflections on those experiences. Throughout this book, I share narratives. I have experienced some of them, whereas in others, I have had to reconstruct to convey the stories of those I have never met, but who play a significant role in my history. My intention is not to feed off of centuries of oppression and exploit these stories. But, that being said, my story would not be complete if I did not acknowledge some of the unsavory parts of this history. I want to unfold the many parts of Haiti through its culture, history, and its people. That is why this is a book of poetry.

In poetry, there are no imposters. Poetry does not pretend to know it all because the writer of the poems does not know it all. Throughout this book, you will find that I ask questions that I wish I could respond to, but I invite you take part in the reflection process with me. I invite you to think, reflect, and even research because we do not know it all. In this collection, I attempt to do two things: ask the questions, and tell you about the country I love and people I love. Some of the stories are gut-wrenching, and others are heart-warming. This book is an immigrant story for immigrants by an immigrant. Even so, can we all not relate to feeling out of place in an environment we wished to fit within? At some point, maybe you have been the outsider. I will explore this feeling through personal experiences of feeling like "the other." Although these poems are personal, the experiences are universal. So regardless of where you come from, all I ask of you, reader, is to see myself in you.

Happy reading,
Laura

I
CULTURE

ONE OF MANY

This is a story of an ordinary man.

He would wake just as the sun's rays stretched to greet him.
He would spend time baking in its warm glow.
Then he would strap his mule to the rusty plow his father
    passed down to him.

After the day's work,
The man would return home.
He would greet his wife.
He would play with his children.
Then he would feed his chickens.

That was the story of this ordinary man.
It was not supposed to change.
It was not supposed to become hectic
Or even mildly interesting.

But we know how the story goes.
He soon wanted more.
Wanted to veer from routine.

Soon enough,
The ordinary man no longer saw himself as such.
His life changed and when he looked around,
He was one of many.

POV

Assuming the worst is our first inclination.
It is only natural we see the world from our coerced,
    microscopic view.

From this narrow lens,
We fix our gazes on arresting stories.
The most sensational.
The ghastliest details.

That is no way to measure a nation.
— No way to value my people.

We are more than shallow accounts.
The depths of our narratives depict more nuanced tales.

Digging deeper,
A people of fighters and wishful dreamers emerge their
    hidden dwelling.
They are valiant successors of generations who came before.

Zoom out of your scaled perspective.
Broaden your scope.

CORNROWS

Don't touch my hair.

These small plaits that lay flat on my scalp are cornrows.

Keep your "boxer braids."
Don't cutesy up their name.

They are cornrows.

They are not a souvenir from our Caribbean excursions.

Their history is profound.
Painful.
Inspiring.

Mothers would drop the seeds of their labor between the
    greased tresses of their daughters' braids.
They made sure that their daughters wouldn't go hungry.

Those little girls were never seen again.

Wives would adopt the style of their husbands' tribes.
They made sure to preserve the traditions etched
    between rows.

Fitting in was crucial.

Leaders would trace intricate patterns into women's scalps.
They made sure their people would find their way home.

Those cornrows were roadmaps that paved the way for freedom.

So, when I say don't touch my hair,
I mean…

Don't mock my ancestry.
Don't disrespect the sacrifice.
Don't forget the paths they paved.

CROWNED

This crown of mine that sits high above,
Claiming her seat on my dome,
Had a long journey before she got there.

She may not be mine,
But the history embedded within her speaks for us both.

Before my time,
The women long ago styled their hair to showcase
    their roots.

You saw a woman whose plaits swept to one side and knew
    where she came from.

You saw one whose plaits formed such elaborate
    patterns that you were sure she belonged with the
    neighboring tribe.

You saw another whose plaits went straight down her scalp
    and knew she was one of you.

Colonists attempted to seize those traditions.
They told the women that it was "just hair."
These settlers wanted to justify quashing their identities.

But the women were fierce.
The women would not let them dare.

So, when I see this crown on my head,
I thank these women.
They preserved a legacy they did not even know was being established.

REFLECTION

As I stare at my reflection in the crystal-clear waters of
    Jacmel,[2]
I am transported back in time.

... To a time when Pétion[3] championed for my freedom.
... To a time when Dessalines'[4] ferocity gained my liberty.
... To a time when Flon's[5] talent yielded my flag.

Though our oppressors sought to tear us down,
Christophe's[6] resourcefulness brought us back up.
Now,
I am transported to the winding hills of the Citadelle
Where his protection still stands, and my people shelter
    in peace.

Though our oppressors sought to silence our tongue,
Morisseau-Leroy's[7] persistence kept our lips moving.
Now,
I am transported to the intricate sounds of my language

---

2   Coastal town in southern Haiti.
3   Alexandre Pétion: Haitian president who pioneered democracy on the island and led British and Spaniard colonizers out of Haiti 1798.
4   Jean-Jacques Dessalines: Haitian founding father and lieutenant, nicknamed "the Tiger."
5   Catherine Flon: Sewed the first Haitian flag in 1803.
6   Henri Christophe: Haitian president known for the construction of the Citadelle Laferrière.
7   Félix Morisseau-Leroy: Poet and advocate for the recognition of Haitian Creole as an official language in Haiti.

Where I say "s*ak pase!*" and my people respond,
   "*n ap boule!*"

Though our oppressors sought to quell our rhythm,
Destiné's[8] imagination sustained our sound.
Now,
I am transported to the echoes of the drums
Where our people move to the melody's beat.

As I stare at my reflection in the crystal-clear waters
   of Jacmel,
I see Faubert[9] and Danticat.[10]
— The women whose prose and intellect enlightened the
   complexities of their time.
Their words transport me to a world that had yet to catch
   up to their outlook on life.

Long before them,
Garoute's[11] suffrage pioneered the path for their ink to hit
   paper
And for their literature to hit the press.

This is the history of my people.

---

8   Jean-Léon Destiné: "Father" of professional Haitian choreography who brought traditional Haitian dance and music to the mainstream.
9   Ida Faubert: Notable Haitian poet.
10 Edwidge Danticat: Considered to be one of the youngest successful Haitian authors, publishing her first works as a teen.
11 Alice Garoute: Haitian suffragette who championed for women's rights.

These are the reasons why when I stare at my reflection in
    the crystal-clear waters of Jacmel,
I don't see myself.

I see her.
I see him.
Because all I am is a reflection of them.

2 TRUTHS AND A LIE

Let's play a little game.
— One of truth and lies.

The native Taínos are the founding inhabitants of the land we know today.
They saw the beauty of its mountainous peaks and named her Ayiti.
But a great man by the name of Columbus fathered the motherland of our people.

This country flourishes with a rich tradition.
Their people value their culture and prolong their diverse heritage.
But the nation is only made up of one race.

A man by the name of L'Ouverture[12] led a whole nation to freedom.
That nation set the precedence for all those who sought the same liberty.
But America is the real champion of anti-slavery.

Truth and lies.
That is the world we live in.

The most blatant deceptions are unequivocally accepted
— Their roles already cemented in our history.

---

[12] Toussaint L'Ouverture: Former Haitian slave who led the slave revolution and continued to lead as a military general.

Yet, the sincerest realities fall to the wayside
— Their veracity struggling to catch up to years of deceit.

But that's the world we live in
— One of truth and lies.

The choice is ours to decide which reality holds the most candor.

MUTUAL HATE

We have settled on a mutual hate for our neighbors.

One stemming from refusal to recognize our distinctions
    and rejoice in our parallels.

A land once united,
Now divided.

Perhaps time is to blame
For it has allocated the years for separation to fester.

Yet in that same span, evolution has occurred in those
    now-partitioned nations.

Though some of our descendants are one in the same,
Time has given way for new traditions to surge.

So, who are we to claim another's identity?
— Tell them who they are?

Our nations were once united.
Now they are divided.

Why must this be cause for this hate to linger?

GOLDEN FLOWER

Rich in pigment was her native Taíno complexion.
Her beauty never claiming credit for her notoriety.

She is the one called Golden Flower.

Projected was her voice as angelic song traveled across
    the village.
Her body moving to the rhythmic beat of drums that
    accompanied her melodies.

She is the one called Golden Flower.

Expressive was her language to craft artistic ballads that
    served as bookmarks for the culture's history.
Her narrative compositions crowning her the poet queen
    of Ayiti.

She is the one called Golden Flower.

Brave she was known as chieftain of a diminishing tribe
    threatened by colonization.
Her peaceful nature uniting a nation torn by pride
    and insurrection.

She is the one called Golden Flower.

Insatiable was the greed of settlers who fought to
    dismantle her integration.
Her adversaries sealing her fate at the hands of a man who
    feared her reign.

She is the one called Golden Flower.

Powerful is the message of courage and dignity
    she imparts.
Her legacy transcending those who sought to see her fall.

She is the one called Anacaona.[13]

---

13   Taino poet and chief of Xaragua, present day Léogâne, Haiti

BY THE VICTORS

From the beginning, we have only known of our people,
    our past through what has been written.
Who were we to question what we'd been told?
  Generations before us had too believed the written word.

Yet, our idleness grew wary.
Our thirst for truth intensified and could not be quenched.

We knew there was more to be uncovered beneath
    the bylines of the authors who claimed to know
    our heritage.
Over time, we learned that some of their pens were tainted
    with the ink of bitterness that would never sweeten.

Were we fools to have been misled by their prose for
    so long?
Suppose our history was not composed by those who
    caused our woes?
What more could we have known?

THE ONES THEY CALL BOAT PEOPLE

Aboard you go!

The "promised land"
Your beacon of hope amongst the turmoil you seek
    to escape.

I cannot pretend to have endured your dismay.
My afflictions amount to nothing next to yours.

You were leaving behind the place you call home.

But in this home,
Your people were slain.
Your expectations of a strengthened economy shattered.
Your once-bountiful lands now rampant with poverty.

So, aboard you went!

Not for animosity towards your people and that land.
But for the ones you held dearest.

Once aboard, did you see the fear behind each other's eyes?
You knew the tales of those who did not make it.
Did you ponder whether this time, it could be you?

The seas were not merciful to your plight.

They agitated your spirits with every uncertain mile of
    your journey.
Some met their last breath, swallowed by the vastness of
    the waters.

Few made it, but not as far as they hoped.
The price of their sacrifice?
Questioning and detainment,
Only to be told they would have to return.

Was the journey then in vain?

The rest evaded detection.
These are the ones they called boat people.

Does such title fit the risk-takers who bear the name?
Do they not deserve the chance to define themselves?

NAME CALLING

I have heard this country called many things.
 Often by those never seeing the glory of its treasures.

To those ignorant ones,

Call it birthplace of the boat people.
Call it epicenter of disaster.
Call it place of worship for that practice with one too many
 "o's."

This land and its people are no strangers to name calling.
So call it what you please,
I will continue to call it home.

DEPLETED

At times,
I am curious of the outcome if our terrain had nothing to offer but dry land.
Would the interest to displace by the masses be inevitable?

A land with no dense forests.
Fields with no sugar canes.
Soil with no precious stones.

Is it still desirable?

But I do not get to live in this world of fantasy.
I do not get to imagine the outcome of this world.
History tells the course of events.

Settlers unrooted the once-lofty barks.
Harvested the juices from the nectars of those stalks.
Dug deep to mine the precious stones.

They continued to do so until the labor proved no longer profitable.

Our land is now depleted.
The yield of our crops has slowed.
Our once-fertile soil, now barren.

How I long to see the restoration of this place to its initial copious state.

TASTES OF HAITI

Season the rice.
Grind the garlic.
Blend the pumpkin.

And you will taste the food of my people.

A rich profile of flavor melding to create delectable meals.

Taste the diri djon djon.
Taste the epis.
Taste the soup joumou.

These are the foods of my people.

SOUNDS OF HAITI

Beat the drum.
Strum the guitar.
Tune the sax.

And you will hear the sounds of my people.

A unique blend of rhythms joining to create
    harmonious melodies.

Hear the jazz.
Hear the twoubadou.
Hear the kompa.

These are the sounds of my people.

PAINT ME A PORTRAIT

Paint me a portrait of Haiti.

Coat your brush
With rich emerald and jade
With citrine and gold
With aquamarine and sapphire.

Dip your brush and paint me this portrait of Haiti.

These are the hues you will need to capture
The richness of her flora
The brilliance of her rays
The depth of her waters.

Fill your canvas with the glistening gems of this land.

PEARL OF THE ANTILLES

Expansive crystal waters.
Lanbi on charcoal.
Children untethered from the weight of garments.
That is life on the island they used to call
Pearl of the Antilles.

A PEOPLE OF NATURE

My people are people of nature.

From the leaves of the plants we sprout,
We remedy.
We use their medicinal qualities to restore in a way only
    they could enable.

From the bark of the trees we grow,
We heal.
We grind their thick skin into a smooth paste to protect us
    from the sun's harsh rays.

From the roots of the lands we cultivate,
We thrive.
We harvest our labor to harness the power of
    God's creation.

We are people of nature.

From the lands we sowed,
We continue to grow.
We refuse to plateau.

WHEN IT RAINS

The rain does not stop our people from working.

When it pours,
Cultivators continue to harvest.
Their shoes fill with red mud from fertile earth

When it pours,
The children continue to frolic,
Their heads tilt up and stick their tongues out to catch the
    cool droplets from the gray skies.

When it pours,
Life goes on.

No, the rain does stop our people.
It nourishes their crop.
It replenishes their spirits.

After the stormy clouds part,
An arc of shades colors the sky and the rays of sunshine
    remind them
There is one who looks down on them as
Life goes on.

A HOSPITABLE PEOPLE

We are a hospitable nation.
We welcome those with whom we have no relation.

We find unity in what divides.
Love takes no sides.

From grounds that produce vegetation that flourish,
We gather to reap their fruit that nourish.

As we learn of the hardships of long ago,
We worry our progress thus far has been too slow.

At this moment, the reparations seem too vast.
But we know they too will be things of the past.

With our love for the land,
We walk together, hand in hand.

Our solidarity does not stem from bloodlines
Our bond escapes any confines.

COUNTRYSIDE

Through the eyes of the artist whose brush strokes capture
    its serenity,
I see a beautiful land.

A lush land, abundant with
Towering palms,
Creamy avocados,
Succulent mangoes.

I see a land with a vibrant sun whose heat never seems
    to burn.

In this land,
 Women wear long skirts and carry their children on
    their backs,
Still, they manage to place a basket of their day's work on
    their heads.

It's okay because it grounds them.
They are used to it.

In this land,
Men work in the fields,
Futilely towing the old mule, inherited from fathers.

Beads of sweat trickle down their faces, as their thin, straw
    hats prove to be no match for the shining rays of that
    vibrant sun.

It's okay because it grounds them.
They are used to it.

In this land,
Children run free over fine grains of sand,
Unconstrained by the pending worries of adulthood.

Amidst the serenity of the countryside,
The current of the river gently whispers to them,
Grounding them,
Comforting them.

CITYSIDE

The city speaks to me differently.

To me, she is truly the one who never sleeps.

The rooter's sunrise crows
Almost fool you into believing you've awoken where mules roam free.

In those short moments, things seem settled.
Dare I say quiet.

You take a deep stretch and savor it.

But it doesn't last long.

Soon,
The serenity vanishes.

The city begins to sing her own tune.

The cars sputter.
The merchants exchange.
The children scream.

The powerlines droop low, but their towers stand tall.
In spite of packed crowds, the city stands out.

The square homes extend beyond the eye's horizon.

Their vibrant exteriors meld into the vivid crescent of color
 that fills the sky after rainfall.

As darkness looms,
The city's lights uncover the shadows of night.

And though she never sleeps,
The city speaks to me differently.

Through the bustling clamor,
I see familiar faces.
I hear the songs of my people.
I smell the dough from the patés in the market.

These are the ordinary dimensions of the city.

Amidst the chaos,
These are the things that keep me grounded.

BLACKOUT

Any given moment presents opportunity
For darkness to engulf the glow of flickering light.

That was life in Haiti.
We'd gotten used to it.

As children,
We would even look forward to it.

In the dark,
You have no distraction.
No scripted characters to fill the silence you can't bear
Left to your own devices.

In the dark,
Your mind is your sole muse.

We were forced to be more imaginative.

We'd hold races to see who could navigate the dark maze
    our living room became.
We'd tell stories overheard from our aunt and uncles.
We'd make up our own tales.

When the fun was over,
The darkness lingered.
Our thoughts were all that remained.

The silence returned and with it, a tranquil presence.
It seeped into my thoughts.
It cloaked my worries.

Today, I chase the stillness of that darkness.
I close my eyes and hope my vision is blanketed with its opacity.
But the glow of light radiates through.

Nothing compares to the darkness in Haiti
That illuminated my mind.

LOVE AND HATE

The way Haitian mothers raise daughters.
I love it.
I hate it.

On one hand,
They ponder their mistakes and make every effort,
So their daughters do not sustain the misfortunes
    they experienced.

They teach their daughters of women whose sacrifices laid
    the foundation for progress.

They show the tough love their daughters need to endure a
    society with no sympathy for their weaknesses.

I am grateful for this.

Yet, Haitian mothers have a way of casting a silent,
    judgmental glare that magnifies their daughters'
    prevailing self-doubt.

They coddle their sons to grow into socialized toddlers
    while their daughters are left to be labeled "too
    emotional."

They invade their daughters' privacy on the premise of
    baseless suspicions.

Unknowingly, they have only supplied their daughters with the tools to construct an impenetrable wall of emotion that prevents anyone getting too close.

All in the name of preserving the fabricated image of the "perfect Haitian daughter."
This infuriates me.

They can be so critical,
Preferential,
Intrusive.

Yet, at their core, Haitian mothers are
Understanding,
Impartial,
Protective.

For that, we love them.

INTERGENERATIONAL

In the beginning, our people were different.
Our mothers and fathers knew who we wanted to be.
And we gathered by a uniting flame to hear who we were.

We laughed.
Danced.
Prayed.

And on the land, we grew.

Life was easier when we knew exactly who we were.
We knew where we belonged.
So, we thrived.

But times changed.

Foreigners seized our land and claimed it as their own.

We plowed the fields and saw the land flourish.
But we never reclaimed it as ours.
We couldn't.

They divided families.
And in doing so, severed our roots.
At least the children's names became easier to pronounce.

Our willpower was stunted by desperate attempts to cling to our knowledge, culture, and identity.

Nevertheless, our stories persevered.

The ones we used to tell brought joy.
But the ones we now told evoked pain.

We heard of our father's torture.
We heard of our mother's heartbreak.
We heard of our own shame.

The very stories we needed to tell inadvertently brought
    about an ache.
Is that the price to pay?

A mind in constant disarray,
Born from an embedded intergenerational wound,
Whose shock remains on our radar.

What's to heal these living scars?

BLEMISH

A nation, once untarnished by the misfortunes of
    the world,
Finds its skin blemished.
Tainted by the civil dissension of a people whose beliefs do
    not align.
Though they have grown apart,
Their love for the land remains.
It is that fondness for the motherland that is able to repair
    the damage that has been done.

HAITI CHERIE,

Home to the soil that sprouts rich Arabica beans destined
    for export, remember,
Always and forever, you will be in my heart.
Invisible is the hope I hold dear for the restoration of
    your terrains.
Triumphant are the ones who liberated a people whose
    only value was their labor, yet their
Infinite fortitude shepherded their path of perseverance.

Crystal blue are your waters that stretch along the shores.
Hear my letter to you,
Embrace these words I write for you.
Resilient are the ones who reside your land, yet know,
Irreplaceable is my attachment for the place I call home
    and though I am beyond your borders,
Endless my love for you, Haiti cherie.

II

IMMIGRATION

THE UNKNOWN

Perhaps the most terrifying part of venturing into the unknown is
The realization that time
Will not stop for us to become accustomed to the change.

FINAL GOODBYE

Saying my goodbyes were easy.

I didn't understand the tears that streamed from my aunts' eyes.
I didn't know why my grandmother held me so tight.
I didn't realize ten years would go by before I would see them again.

To live in ignorant bliss.

I was oblivious to the bureaucratic restraints that would keep my family apart.
I had hopes that the thing I dreamed of most was finally coming true.

I was fixated on a better future,
And certain the rest of my family was soon to be reunited.

Goodbyes seemed trivial.

I should have known better than to keep existing in the realm of fantasy that only prevailed in my mind.

I wish I could go back to that day.
I wish I cried with them.
I wish I held on to my gran and never let go.

I wish I realized that, for us,
It would be our final goodbye.

A CONVERSATION BETWEEN A MOTHER AND A DAUGHTER

Manmi, where do we actually come from?
>I wish I knew, cherie,
>But our people were taken from the place they used to call home.
>We had to rebuild here.

Manmi, what do you dream about?
>Only that we have each other forever and that we're happy.

Manmi, what makes you sad?
>Only knowing that I won't be there to protect you forever.

What would they say about me?
>Only that you are different than them.

Manmi, so how do I be more like them?
>...

CLOUD NINE

I had fantasized about an America I didn't
    truly understand.

This America put me on cloud nine.

I dreamed of a people who molded a rainbow of peach and
    brown tones.

I dreamed of bringing my teacher an apple on the first day
    like I had seen in those movies.

I dreamed of a people who yearned to learn my language
    as much as I aspired to know theirs.

In my America,
I was content. I was successful.

My family was united under one roof, and all our burdens
    were lifted.

I felt safe.
I felt welcomed.

In this America that I had fantasized,
I was home.

BOARDING

My mother looks down.
She motions for me to rise.
My legs tremble with anticipation as the unknown
    approaches closer.
We were to embark on the journey that would change it all.

ARRIVAL

On this cold evening,
I reminisce on the moments of the past.
Curiosity for the future that awaits orbit those moments
To a place soon to be lost in time.

BECOME A SPONGE

I don't recall the instant I began to soak it in.

There were others in the classroom
— They too were absorbing.

They too were taken from their seats.
"Ready for your special lessons?"
The teachers would ask.

My eyes would frantically dart from left to right.
I would tentatively find my way to the door.
I didn't feel special at all.

In the beginning, the words floated aimlessly about
Unable to permeate my mulish brain.

I refused to open up,
Hoping to hold on to the words I risked losing.

Eventually, I grew porous.
I was more inclined to let the foreign phrases in.

When at home,
I spoke my mother tongue and the foreign words would
    elude me.

I thought I was shriveling up.

But every time, I would return,

I would absorb it all again.

That's how I learned to speak this foreign tongue.

The key,
I noticed,
Was to become a sponge.

To soak it all in.

It served me well for a while.

BECOME A SPONGE, PT. 2

It served me well for a while
— Becoming a sponge.

Soaking in everything they wanted me to learn.

Observe. Practice. Retain.

It served me well.
Until it didn't.

Soon enough,
I was observing, practicing, retaining.
And applying.

Applying not only what they wanted me to learn,
But the underlying behaviors they wanted me to adopt.

I gave in.
It was what was expected.
I molded my conduct to align with theirs.

I mirrored the way they spoke.
— Adapting to their vernacular and managing to weasel
    "like" into every sentence.

I mirrored the way they learned.
— Reciting speeches and pouring over my Haitian history
    textbooks were ways of the past.

I mirrored the way they ate.
— Preferring the indulgence of fast food over my mother's homecooked meals.

And once I fell down that adverse path of imitation,
I was nothing more than a shriveled sponge.
Hoping for the right matter to make me anew.

Lost in despair.
A broken identity was born,
That took years to repair.

IT

My fingers followed the path *it* ingrained in my skin.

For years, I covered *it* up.
I would instinctively reach for my sleeve as a veil for the insecurity and discomfort.
Made sure to conceal *it* because questions are all *it* would incur.

"What is that?"
"Did you get burned?"
"It means you're not from here, right?"

It was a magnet for curiosity
— Only attracting unwarranted acknowledgment.

I believed there to be no alternative than discretion.
I blamed *it* for a lot.

It told the world the narrative I had yet to divulge.

That I don't belong.
That I would have to prove myself.

It told the world who I was.

As inconspicuous as *it* was,
It spoke volumes before I had a chance to mutter my name.

For years, I resented *it*.

I hated how people looked at *it* before meeting my gaze.

I knew in those moments,
They thought they knew who I was.

But the more I saw others with it, the more my own misgivings quelled.

I could trace along the etched impression unencumbered by insecurity and discomfort.

I knew that I was not alone.

That is the power of this obscure mark.
That is the power of *it*.

CALLING CARDS

My father would roll down his window and wait for an attendant to arrive.
He would send my sister and me into the cramped corner store to restock on our weekly cards.

Those cards were our only link to family in the early days.

My sister and I would roam the narrow aisles to extend our trip.
We would run our fingers against the bags of chips, just to hear their crinkle.
Then we would make our way to the front where the cards were all along.

We would always leave with the plain, red Boss Revolution in tow.

When we got home,
I would find a coin and scratch off the sealant
To reveal the long string of numbers that would connect us to our loved ones.

We all huddled by the phone
— Never knowing how long we would have before our words would be cut short.

I had memorized the robotic operator cadence on the line as she listed our options.
We'd press the # for the tenth time.

It was a lengthy process.

It was worth it,
Because I knew that as soon as the call connected,
My grandmother's voice would replace the mechanized monotone.

Just as our conversations would move past pleasantries,
The call would drop.
There would always be much left unsaid.

OUR REASONS

We all had a reason —
A moment that made us wonder if there was a life better
    than the one we were afforded.

Some needed to escape the turmoil of violence and
    insecurity
That robbed us of our sleep.

Some looked around our humble stations
And wondered if greener pastures were ahead.

Some peered into the hopeful eyes of children they raised
And aspired for their views to encompass greater optics.

We all had a reason.

Some of us thought of our country.
Some of us thought of our livelihood.
Some of us thought of our children.

But we're bound with the same intention to pursue
Something bigger than ourselves.

INSIDE JOKE

Krik?

Krak!

They told her she was coming to a land of opportunities but forgot to mention she wouldn't be offered any of them.

Hahaha

Krik?

Krak!

They told her her hair would look better straight but forgot to mention even straightened, her kinky coils wouldn't catch the wind.

Hahaha

Krik?

Krak!

They told her that English would be key to her new way of life but forgot to mention her mother and father would never be ready to give up her native tongue.

Hahaha

Krik?

Krak!

They told her she was too different from the rest of the pack, but she forgot to mention that she was done carrying all of their burdens on her back.

Hahaha

MICROAGGRESSIONS

You're so well-spoken for...

— a little girl who spent thirty hours reading every week?
I guess that explains it.

But you don't look like...

— the product of a country whose people create an ethnic
   mosaic of culture and diversity?
I guess we do tend to look a little different.

But I thought your people...

— were the first in the Western Hemisphere to break
   from the chains that were intent on keeping us within
   our bounds?
I guess we're trendsetters.

Trust me, you're not like the rest of them...
— Trust me, I am.

Well, at least you'd make a great nurse.

SCAPEGOAT

I am not your scapegoat.

Not the one to blame,
For taking the jobs that bring you shame.

I am not your victim.

I will not sit idly by within a system this size,
Determined never to see me rise.

I am not your refuge.

Stop unpacking your ache like a perpetual deluge.
The burdens on my back are already huge.

We work hard to pave our own path.
We are the sons and daughters of a bloodline that
    never fails.
We are no longer beholden to the guilt you feel for
    witnessing our tragedies.

We are not your anything.

7.0

January 12, 2010.
I did nothing that day but pray and cry, amen.

My people were held captive under a pile of rubble.
Nothing could be done as I watched their world crumble.

7.0
That's all it took for Marie to become a widow.

The disaster of the decade.
I was overwhelmed with guilt to have been left unscathed.

Now that my city was the epicenter,
No one spoke of her past splendor.

For days, bodies lined the street.
To claim loved ones was no small feat.

We tirelessly called to connect.
But the lines would interject.

We called to ensure they found shelter.
But our worries continued to fester.

We called to know if we still had a family.
Yet, all was unknown through the calamity.

250,000 lives.
It's painful to grasp, but their legacy survives.

A GIRL WITH MANY HATS

I donned many hats into adolescence.

You could call it the downside of nailing English.

My mother would sit at the dining table
With a mountain of papers waiting to be read.
She'd shuffle them around for a while, but
It was ultimately up to me to translate them.

My mother would lie on the couch
With a blank screen waiting to be turned on.
She'd press some buttons for a while, but
It was ultimately up to me to turn the static into an image.

My mother would sit at the doctor's office
With a list of prescriptions waiting to be filled.
She'd stare at it for a while, but
It was ultimately up to me to speak up.

I was a translator.
I was a fixer.
I was an advocate.

For years, I donned those hats.

But, for much longer,
My mother donned countless others.

SACRIFICES

A little piece of paper is all you had to sign.
Suddenly, all was left behind.

You withdrew from the life you knew,
To immerse yourself in a world that was new.

The faces of the ones you love most,
Replaced by tiny screens as your only dose.

In your country, you follow your passion.
Now, your job's only worth a paycheck to cash in.

I knew you felt isolated.
You feared revealing your culture would leave you berated.

You still educated us on who we were,
From our culture, we would never deter.

Through your relentless dedication,
We were able to receive a great education.

Your sacrifices didn't go unnoticed.
For them, I remain focused.

You didn't come here to make a better life for you.
You came to afford a brighter future for us two.

FORWARD IN REVERSE

We lived like kings and queens in the motherland.

We went to the best schools,
Had people who catered to us.
Jobs were plentiful.

In our eyes, it was not enough.
The prospect of something greater festered, a hunger that would only be satiated by abandoning all we had known.
We did just so —
For a life that put us in the lowest ranks of society.

To think that is prospect of "better opportunities" we assumed would satiate our hunger…

Are we fools to assume we'd still live like kings and queens?

We couldn't have known what was in store.

In this pursuit from rags to riches,
We seemed to do the opposite.

Our children now attended the nearest public school available.
We became the ones who catered.

The roles had reversed.
And there was no going back.

DREAM ON

We come into a foreign world attempting to claim it as our own
Because they told us we could.

Yet it was never divulged that this world would inherently reject us.
Polarize us.

Even so,
We desperately grasp at the hopes of a Dream
We are told would be the quintessential denotation of success.

Come here.
Go to school.
Get good grades.
Go to school again.
Get better grades, a better job, and you'll see a better life.

Sounds easy enough.

What they forgot to mention is the Dream is nearly unattainable for most of us.

The Dream,
Yes,
The one uniquely crafted for you and me is out of reach.

Imagine that.

MIRAGE

A mythic place shaped by the oblivion of optimism.
We buy into the narratives this place builds.

We blindly sing odes to its pledges.
Those of life.
Liberty.
Happiness.

Reality quickly deconstructs the wishful vows of this place.
Bares its truth for our gaze.

How quick we were to believe
In this mythic world that sold nothing but empty dreams.

OUR OWN WORST ENEMY

We are offered the blueprint of the Dream on a
    silver platter.

But we are no longer blind to its false pretenses.
So, we reject the Dream entirely.

But it proves to be a harder feat.
— Rejecting it, I mean.

We hope to hold on to the slightest hope that we may be
    the exception.
So, the Dream persists.

In the moments where it presents its faults,
We are our sole adversary.

There is no society to blame.
No institutional policies on which to unburden our woes.

In the moments when we are able to dismantle the Dream
— Accept it as the mere façade that it is —
We are our own worst enemy.

That in itself is hard to grasp.
So, the Dream persists.

AAVE

From a young age, we're taught a set of principles.

One that limits our convictions,
Our actions.
Our expressions.

When we deviate from those guidelines, we're chastised
— Told we sound improper.

This "proper speech,"
—One deeply rooted in a suburban upper echelon—
Was never meant for our ears.

Yet, we are being told to calibrate the tune of our ears and
Mimic the defined tone of "colloquial speech" society has
    deemed "proper."

We comply.
We conform and say our lines.
Refusal to do so would bar us from a society that's already
    reluctant
To let us in.

Nowadays, it's engrained in our subconscious.
It's expected that we suppress our speech
—Our identity—
To pursue that which belongs to somebody else.

We're more accessible that way.
We put everyone else at ease.

At what cost?

How long are we meant to forge the Queen's English?

When can we begin to embrace ours?

CRENGLISH

In my new world,
I became accustomed to another vernacular.
With the learned phrases in tow,
I was no longer a passive passenger.

I began to see words jump from the pages of novels I read.
I learned the intricacies of the metaphors.
I delved into understanding the underlying connotations
    of the slang.

But with the competing words of my mother tongue
    floating about,
I felt like a boomerang.

My mother tongue was never too far away.
At home, she would always resurface.
Ready to dominate over the words I'd learned that day.

At times, I would let her.

I anticipated her return when no other words
Could capture the essence of the thoughts that were at
    odds in my head.
I anticipated her return when English words would lack, to
    some extent.

I would find myself weaving her phrases into the English
    I spoke.
In those breaths, the passion in my words did
    not extinguish.

The power of the two languages expanded my platform.
Creole and English.
An unlikely yet divine coupling.

COPING

We all have our ways of coping.

But a commonality lies among us.
We are all shifting puzzle pieces awaiting the gap that
    reveals where we fit in the larger picture.
The one that tells us where we belong.

In the meantime,

Some of us assimilate.
We completely abandon every aspect of the person we were.
We desperately renounce the past to reshape our future.

To those copers, I wish for you to reconnect with a piece of
    that former self.

Some of us separate.
We wholly cling to our culture and attach to every facet of
    our past.
We hesitantly adapt to the ways of our unfamiliar
    surroundings as we fear they will claim our identity.

To those copers, I wish for you to open up and see what the
    rest of the world has to offer.

Some of us integrate.
We value the traditions of our people and learn about the
    history of theirs.

We incorporate the parts of our culture that we could not
    bear to lose and adapt to the manners of our new home.

To those copers, I wish for you to stay connected with the
    most genuine parts of you.

Some of us are not afforded a choice.
We do not get to decide whether to assimilate, separate,
    or integrate.

We're wholeheartedly disgraced.
Meant to feel out of place.
Left to yearn for our brothers' warm embrace.

To those copers, I wish for you to be granted the reverence
    you merit.
Know that I hurt, cry, and plead with you.

LOST MEMORIES

The memories I miss most are ones I can't remember at all.

The frightful walk to the schoolyard on the first day of primary school…
The seemingly impossible memorization and recitation of presidential speeches at six years old…
The feeling of the sun's warm rays of my brown skin on a Sunday morning…

I wish I could recall those moments.

Maybe they would provide me with a more profound connection to myself.

I *knew* they happened.
I could *hear* the echoes of these moments as I reminisced on my life before.
At times I could even *feel* them.

Yet the memories still evade me.

I would hear my mother narrate the same stories incessantly.

Somehow, I tricked myself into believing that these moments were my own.
That these memories were my own.

It's hard to differentiate, now, between the memories I hold
And the ones I wish I had.

At times, it seems like they've all been wiped clean.
Like I was given a blank slate for the memories I would
    have to make.

I didn't ask for that.

Relinquishing my memories to a life that I had yet to know.

It doesn't seem like a fair trade.

SILENT THREAT

Memories of what has been
Are always threatened by
Moments that will come to be.

SECRET'S OUT

I made it to the "land of opportunities"
For that,
I am grateful.

But I'm no fool.
I know that since their inception,
Some of these opportunities you claimed were for me,
Were only empty promises.

You took me at face value.
You looked at my documents.
You looked at my clothes.
You looked at my passport.
And that was enough to tell you where I belonged.

Social cohesion, you say.
Racial separation, you mean.

Time deceived us.
These oppressive systems had not gone away.
Real changes were few and far between.

But I know your secret.

You thought we weren't quite right.

But you had a plan.

You would just teach us to write.

But not tell the stories from our birthright.
Only the ones that suited your delight.

You didn't want us close.
So where it mattered most, we were never welcomed.

You knew we had our ways.
But you compelled us to put them out of sight.
Out of mind.

You took your time.
You didn't want us to catch on.

But soon enough,

We seemed alright.
We told the stories you would recite.
We were so polite.

You took your time.

But soon enough,

We forgot our plight.

Your secret's out.

But you still don't care, no doubt.

CIRCLE OF MANIPULATION

We all crave ordinary.
It gives us a sense of normalcy.

We want to know what to expect.
That way, our homogeneous routines don't lose their
    mundane predictabilities.

This is the way society operates.

We believe what we hear,
Because it's what our history books have taught
    for decades.

We reject the stories we dislike,
Because we've been taught that they are not to be trusted.

We think narrowly,
Because we've inherited generations of prejudice to keep us
    in the past.

We don't care if some of these practices are antiquated.
We find comfort in their repetition.

So, we demand these systems to remain unchanged.

We reinforce them to bring ourselves a moment of peace.

We know it pains some of our brothers and sisters.
Yet, we perpetuate these norms.

In reality, we are not ordinary.
Our world is unpredictable.
It is far from peaceful.

Yet still, we continue to bolster the things that give rise to the most hatred.
They are the things we can predict.
They are the things that satiate our need for ordinary.

FALSE HOPE

In this land of the free,

Individualist mindsets supersede.
The notion was to be successful; I'd have to lead.

But I wasn't raised to develop this sense of greed.
My people would have agreed.

Besides, this success they speak of is not guaranteed.

Even for our fundamental rights, we had to plead.
But at last, we were freed.

Yet, we're still treated like a different breed —
Never getting the chance to be brought up to speed.

Most of us felt like we had to concede.

I guess it's true this country was never set up for us
    to succeed.

THE ODDS ARE NOT IN OUR FAVOR

In this land,
We are the minority.

When decisions are made,
We're naught but an afterthought.

They find no shame in enforcing the same norms that have guided their institutions for centuries.

Those principles continue to serve them well.
So, they have no incentive to do so.

In school, we didn't have the option to learn the language of our mothers.

Remember,
We're the minority.

They wouldn't be able to sell our tongue to enough people.

We get through it anyway.
We're used to it.

Some of us level up.

Some of us stay exactly where they expected us to be.

But even those of us who exceeded their expectations
   quickly realize that they continue to fight the
   same battles.
Is it worth it then?

Leveling up only to realize that
The odds are not in our favor?

ALLY

You ask me how to be an ally.

Here's your blueprint:

Don't merely sympathize with my pain.
Cry along with me.

Stop dispersing images that ignite a sharp ache within me.
Work, so I don't have to see them again.

Silence the misconceptions of that conditioned voice in
    your head.
Immerse yourself in a world that challenges you to develop
    a new one.

Drop the forced smile and instinctive reach for your purse.
Realize we are not so far removed from each other as you
    may believe.

Pack up your past transgressions.
Learn from those mistakes and don't repeat them.

Enough with the rumors you saw on your feed.
Grab a copy and educate yourself along with me.

You ask me how to be an ally?

Cry with me.
Work with me.

Walk with me.
Respect me.
Learn with me.
Read with me.

When it matters most,
Show them you still stand with me.

RECONCILIATION

For centuries, we have fostered a hatred that tore us apart.

Although our roots revealed kinship,
Our love for one another was conditional.

We only cared for one another when odds appeared to lean in our favor.

Other times, we inflicted a pain that wounded our innermost being.
Those were the words that damaged us most.

It all came from a place of hurt that we are internally trying to recuperate.

But we chose the wrong enemies.

We chose our brothers.
We chose our sisters.
We chose ourselves.

We blame them for a fire that none of us set.
Yet, whose elusive flames we continue to rekindle.

It is no way to heal.

If we are meant to repair broken fences that have yet to be mended,
We must start with reconciliation.

We must realize that the fabric of our history is woven
   from the same cloth.
We must realize that our differences are not what
   divides us.
Our uniqueness unifies us.

On our path to reconciliation,
Let us celebrate our successes.
Let us honor our traditions.
Let us heal our affiliation.

On this path, let us love.

OUR ULTIMATE DEMISE

It's disheartening how we don't want to see each other win.
Now, that's truly an iniquitous sin.

To put down our brothers and sisters during their most
    extraordinary highs,
At this rate, we'll be the ones to blame for our
    ultimate demise.

We've grown up in a world that breeds deep oppression.
So why then do we add to this transgression?

Your brother tells you that he's moving on to bigger and
    better things.
Yet all you can do is remind him of the challenge this
    world brings.

Your sister tells you she's finally found the courage to use
    her voice.
Yet you shame her into believing silence is her only choice.

Your grandmother tells you stories of where you're from.
Yet you shut her out, so she doesn't see the person
    you've become.

Don't you know we be better off if we were to reunite?
Band together to reach a new height?

For ages,

We have been placed at a disadvantage that's intent on seeing us fail.
Now,
It is up to us to gather and show that we can prevail.

III
IDENTITY

REGRET

My biggest regret was leaving for so long.

We all say we'll visit every year;
Rarely do we follow through.

I departed from a place I used to call home
To settle in another that I had to make my own.

On that brisk March day I left,
I never imagined it would be another eight years before I returned.

It's a shame, truly.

Countless memories missed.

Goodbyes never spoken.

Guilt felt to have been spared the permanent pain.

When I found my way back,
I landed in a country I barely recalled.

The once familiar backroads became puzzling mazes to navigate.

The school I once attended became yet another unrecognizable structure.

The people who once raised me became mere strangers.

I almost did not feel at home.

It's a shame, truly.

To go from a place you used to call home,
To yearning to return to another that you had to make
    your own.

THE SUPER IMMIGRANTS

Ladies and gentlemen,

May I present to you
The super immigrants.

The ones who were always the topic of conversation at gatherings.
The ones who never had trouble fitting into new crowds.
The ones the world always told us to become.

In a way,

They are saviors.
— Preserving hope for those who still believe.

They are champions.
— Victors of a dream most of us let slip through our fingers.

I saw them as adversaries.
The ones my parents would compare me to.

Never quite fitting in,
I longed for their knack in camouflage.

They set the pace, and we were expected to follow.
I was tired of the burden of living up to their caliber.
But all I really wanted was to be super too.

BITTER

Jealously breeds our ugliest truths.

TEAM EFFORT

Seldom are our accomplishments only our own.

We have the wisdom of our parents to guide the decisions we make.

We have the reinforcement of our brothers and sisters to help bear the weight of risks we take.

We have the animosity of our opposers to ignite the rage that urges us to prove them wrong.

We have the protection of a creator to clear the fog of our blurred visions.

So, my immigration story is not merely my own.

Yours is not only yours either.

How often, though, after we've said "mama, I made it," do we step back and look
To those happy moments
To those people
To those hardships?

And realize no part of journeys would be complete without them.

UNSPOKEN

To be silent but demand to be understood.
That is the way of the unspoken truths.

JUGGLING ACT

Sit pretty.

Stand tall.

Smile wide.

Seems simple enough.

Until it becomes the vain criteria you are expected to satisfy.

It's exhausting.

We have to dress up.
But be careful that you don't show off.

We have to wear makeup.
But be careful that you don't catfish.

We have to be successful.
But be careful that you're not the breadwinner.

All while, you must entertain the mass of spectators demanding you embody that Coke bottle everyone's always talking about.

It's exhausting, see.

GOOD HAIR

I've always wanted that *good hair*.

The one that doesn't get caught in between the narrow spaces of my brush.
The one with curls that spring back up into neat coils after twirling them in between my fingers.
The one from the models whose faces dominated the ads in between my shows.

3A.
3B.
3C.

We were taught that those were the desirable ones.

So we shied away from
4A.
4B.

And sprinted away from the tighter coils of
4C.

These girls didn't have that *good hair*.

I didn't have that *good hair*.

Who told us that anyway?

Who thought it was okay to look at a little girl

And tell her that her hair wasn't that good?

Didn't they know she would end up thinking that *she* wasn't that good?

Our society has a funny way of dealing with these things.

We know that those words hurt.

Yet, we perpetuate those wounding words that we too,
Were told as little girls.

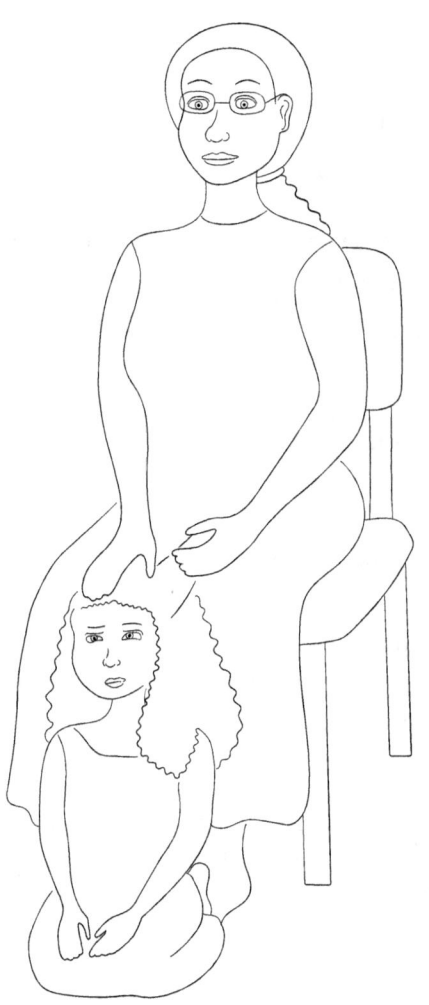

REDEFINED

I told everyone I'd never "go natural."

It's strange how we perceive this innate characteristic of ourselves as unnatural.

Maybe it's because we are tainted with the idea
That only *some* roots were good.

Ours were not.

Good hair sounds complimentary.
Coveted.

Yet, at its mention, my dense coils shrink even tighter.

I want *good hair*.
Not because my curls are loose and easy to manage.
I want it to mean just that,
GOOD hair.

Let me define.

My GOOD hair is…

Bold
Elegant
Artful
Unique
Timeless
Impeccable
Fierce
Untouchable
Lustrous
My GOOD hair is beautiful.

YOUR SMILE SAYS...

Your smile utters the words you could never bring yourself
   to feel.

I watched my grandmother smile to tell me what she never
   could
— Being the aloof introvert that she was.

At seven years old, I was elated to discover I would be
   coming to the land that would fulfill my curiosity.
I would tell my grandmother that we'd send for her soon.
I thought I could snap my fingers and she would be with
   us.
My grandmother gazed off into the distance, and her eyes
   would swell with tears.

Still, she still smiled to spare my child-like wonder.
   because she knew that I was naïve.

At eleven years old, I learned that she was diagnosed
   with dementia.
I would tell my grandmother that she would get
   better soon.
I thought telling her the same stories every week would
   make her remember.
My grandmother grew silent on the phone and fought to
   speak through her headache.

Still, she smiled to preserve my unwavering optimism.

At twenty-one years old, I am finally trying to grieve my
 grandmother's death.
I tell my mother that I had already done it ten years earlier.
I thought not reliving the memories of her would mean
 I would not have to mourn along with the rest of
 my family.
I would write of my woes and hide my sorrows.

Still, I smiled to mask my constant ache.

At last,
I have uncovered the truths of our smiles.

When you smile through your tears, everyone knows you
 are still heartbroken.

When you smile through your pain, everyone knows you
 are still suffering.

When you smile through your fears, everyone knows you
 have yet to overcome them.

THE STORY HER EYES TOLD ME

Your eyes tell a story.
They reveal the truth of the deception you attempt to conceal.
The truth you have perhaps hid from the world.
The truth you hide from yourself.

No words could express my sheer fervor when I learned that
I was soon to live out the Dream.

On the Monday morning that my mother took me to get my passport photos taken,
She outlined a set of rules on how I should behave.

Sit down, politely.
Look straight into the camera.
Don't smile.

And I did just so.

When I got to the studio,

I saw down quietly,
Stared straight into the lens,
And did not move a muscle on my face.
 No gimmicks.

But on the inside, my excitement could barely be contained.

I was certain the camera would capture my joy.

Or so I thought.

Ten years later, I found that 2x2 square tucked beneath a stack of dusty albums.

The seven-year-old girl whose eyes peered into mine lacked all fervor.
Her eyes told a story of pure dread.
Angst.
Insecurity.
Fear.

As I stared into her eyes,
I saw her real story.
The one she did not even realize she was hiding from herself.

Little did she know, she was to be uprooted from her life to relocate to a new country,
A new home.
A new normal.
And she was scared out of her mind.

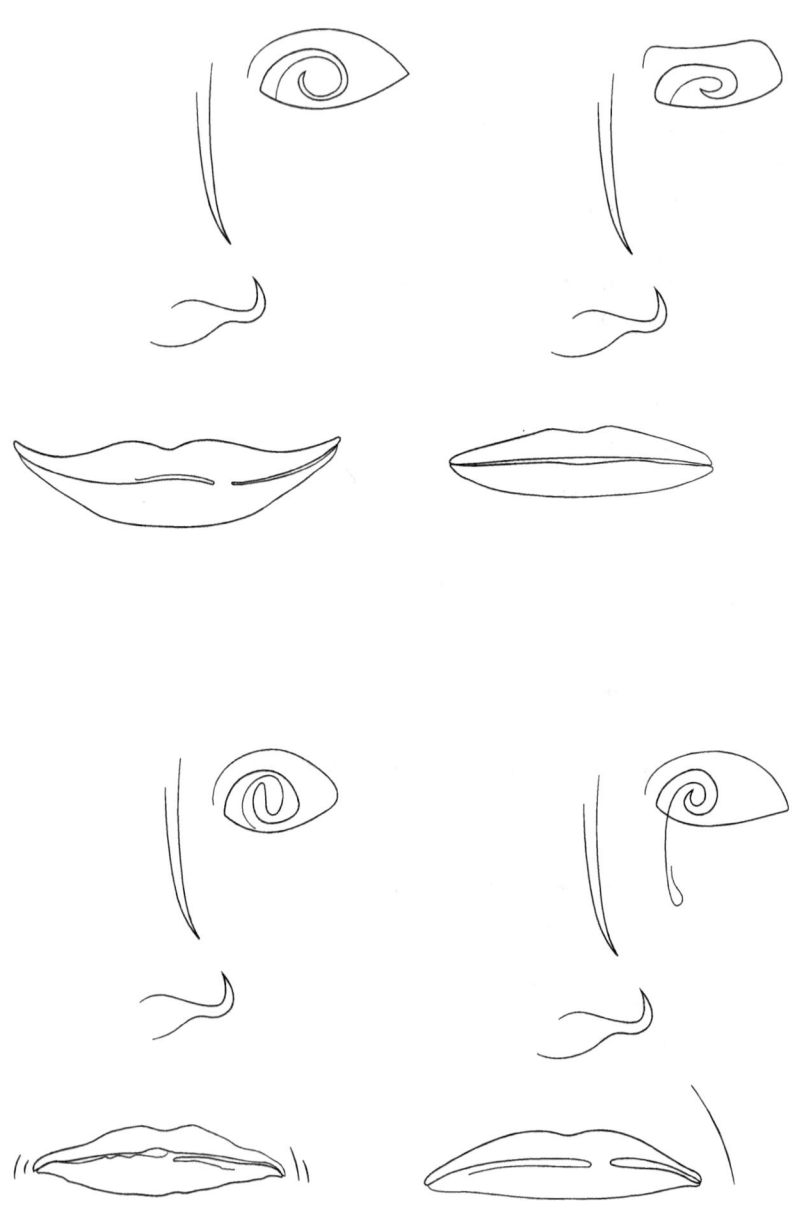

THE STRANGER

I knew a man I would not see often.

He was of average height.
Had a lanky frame.
Always wore oversized slacks.
Was balding and proud of it.

When he'd come around,
We were close.

He would kiss me on the forehead,
Overcompensate with gifts.
And even try to discipline me.
— At that, he rarely succeeded.
Teaching moral foundations to someone you barely knew
    was a hard feat.

I would see him for a few weeks on special occasions,
Then he'd vanish.

This revolving door of a relationship left only a slim gap for
    a close bond to form.
So, I did not know this man well.

Over the years, I grew closer to this stranger.
I learned he loved to cook.
I learned he loved surprises.
I learned how he loved.

Today, I look at this man who I have grown to love.
And wonder how he was ever once a stranger.

I now call him my father.

LOVE LANGUAGE

I did not know my father loved me until I was 16 years old.

Let me explain.

I wasn't tucked in after a blissful bedtime story.
He's a Haitian father, after all.
He doesn't do bedtime stories.

I didn't turn to the stands and see him ornamented in
    school spirit at games, cheering me on.
He's a Haitian father, after all.
He doesn't waste his money on trivial memorabilia.

I never turned to him for help with my menial
    teenage angst.
He's a Haitian father, after all.
He doesn't do well with emotion.

Those three words I longed to hear never came until I was
    16 years old.

He loved differently.

On the days I did not feel like myself, he would shower me
    with all he could find to raise my spirits.

On the nights I could not sleep, he would be my sole
    companion to watch reruns of programs we'd seen
    countless times before.

At the mention of any snack I remotely enjoyed, he would emerge with every flavor I had yet to try.

I did not know my father loved me until I was 16 years old.

But let me explain.

He wanted me to be stimulated by the stories of my own imagination.

He wanted me to understand the one who loves is not always the one who stands out the most.

He wanted me to first validate my feelings by learning to accept myself.

His quiet charisma projected more than his word ever could.
He's a Haitian father, after all.
He was all I needed to keep me grounded.

IN A BUBBLE

The will of a parent is the aspiration of "the best" for
    their children.
I have wondered what this means for them.
Is "the best" a shield of protection from the worst to come?

A mother tells her daughter that she is beautiful.
But her daughter never learns to defend against the ones
    who tell her otherwise.

A father tells his son to treat women with respect.
But his son never learns to confront the friends who do the
    opposite.

My mother put me in a bubble.

She told me I was beautiful.
She told me to love myself.
She told me I could achieve everything I would ever want.

The affirmation from her consolation rang true.
And I took her word for it.

That is until my bubble popped, and the world told
    me otherwise.

I wish she prepared me for that world.
A world that was in on the joke I was never privy to.

If only she had revealed what everyone else saw in me,
	I would be primed to the ugly truth that I would inevitably encounter.

I bet she thought it was "the best."
I doubt she realized she was filling my head with
	sweet nothings.
I am sure she was only projecting a world that saw me in
	the way she did.

A COMPLICATED LOVE STORY

The love I knew before all love was my mother's.

How I wish I could feel her caress in the photos I reminisce over.
— Be taken back to a time where worries did not linger.

A mother and daughter love is complicated.
We long for the treasured memories we share
Just as much as we long to escape the ones we wish weren't there.

Those wavering feelings are complicated.
But that is a mother and daughter love.

Through it all,
I would rather spend the last of my sunrises
Knowing I have less time to be awoken by the warm rays of her love
Rather than watch my days waste away in the cold embrace of an interim lover.

Though this love is complicated,
It is complicated by nothing and no one.

A MIDNIGHT DRIVE-THRU KIND OF LOVE

If mother and daughter love is complicated,
Sister love is inexplicable.

It's telling them to stop squeezing into your clothes
And wearing their boots the next day.

It's arguing about the little things
Only to have the anger surmount to nothing.

It's the knowing glances from across the room.
And the understanding that no one truly apologizes.

Sister love is
Late night drives,
Driving each other crazy,
And drive-thrus at midnight.

TO THE REAL ONES

My soul found peace when it knew I was not alone.
That there were ones there to soothe the unruly patter of
    my center.
To extract truths and tender sorrows.
To bind a friendship
Of hickory roots and delicate leaves.

PASSBERBY

Our greatest anxieties stem from the fears from within.

The ones that no one but us are privy to.

Still, we worry.
Ponder whether others see what we aim to conceal.
Those are the fears that stunt our growth.

If only we could see the indifference of others,
Perhaps we would accept that we are all mere passersby
Making brief stops into each other's lives.

IN MY HEAD

I shouldn't have said that.

What are they going to think?
Are they looking at me?
Was that good enough?
Am I good enough?
I ask myself in solitude.

You shouldn't have done that.
They *are* judging you.
They *are* staring at you.
You *did* not do good enough.
You *are* not good enough.

I tell myself in solitude.
Stop.
Get out of my head.

Start to run.
After a while, the surroundings seem familiar.
I look for my opponents but am the sole competitor.
The course is endless yet leads back to me.

To my friends, I am vigilant.
To my teachers, I am observant.
To my parents, I am just fine.

Why then is it impossible cross to the finish line?
Why then do I try to escape myself?

Why then do I attempt to silence the burdens of my own mind.
Why then do they only scream louder?

FORESIGHT

I see a scared girl.
She stares back, and her pupils dilate.
I am entranced by the auspicious foresight her eyes present.
Through her gaze, all I have desired is illuminated.
So, I sink into the obsidian doors they open.

AN ESCAPE

Sometimes this doesn't feel real.
We constantly try to conceal the parts we are meant to heal.
But this reparation we strive to feel is not mended in our minds made of steel.

We combat our separation only with aggravation.
We should be fostering dedication to communication and collaboration.
This is not the way of this generation that is quick to submit to resignation.

Yet, availing oneself in reality begins through reconciling with society.

Why then do we try to shelter our thoughts from each other?
Standing together, we would progress much further.

Instead,

We've stunted our growth.

In doing so,

We no longer feel.
We've lost our zeal.
And we continue to conceal.

So as not to face the parts that feel too real.

BETWEEN THE SOMETHINGS

In our teens, we chase the looming presence
  of adolescence.
In our twenty-somethings, we flee the liabilities
  of adulthood.
What will become of our thirty-somethings?
When do we begin to live for the moments between the
  "things"?

INTROSPECTION

On your quest for answers,
Look inward.
With questions you wish you could answer about yourself.

OREO

Let's get this straight.

No, I'm not from the valley because my pitch fluctuates
    when I interact with you.
I'm not trying to "sound white."

My friends may not look like all of yours.
That doesn't make me a sellout.

Black women are used to being compared to food.

So, I see where your reference comes from.

Why does what you see on the outside,
Make you assume who I am on the inside?

I'm no different than who I say I am.

And I will not be defined by who you claim me to be.

But I guess I missed the course that taught me to be black.

My mistake.

INTERSECTIONALITY

When asked who I am and who I want to be,
I contemplate the person I will choose to be.

Never did it cross my mind that it was a choice I did not
have to make.

Unearthing the layers of my being,
I discover the individuality of the parts that summarily
are me.

I am a daughter.
A Haitian.
An immigrant.
A writer.

Am I inauthentic if I choose not to share the other layers
with you?

And when asked who I am and who I want to be,
Must I choose only one piece to tell you who I am?

I am just ordinary.

ABSPORTION

When things looked as though they were going to
  fall apart,

I would close my eyes and allow the darkness to absorb the
  qualms.

The longer I kept them shut, the deeper I sunk into a realm
  that existed somewhere only I knew.

A WELCOMED OASIS

At times, I found myself submitting to the alluring
   familiarity of the Dream I seldom wanted
   to acknowledge.

It was the welcomed oasis I sought for solace.
It was comforting to stay there
Until darkness swept away the recurring nightmares of the
   unknown.

So, I would keep my eyes closed.

When I woke, I wondered why I had stayed for too long.
What was there left to chase in that dark abyss?

For fear of the unknown,
I would take the easy way out.
I would blame the Dream.

Entering the maze of its promises was tempting.
Knowing it would be difficult to find my way out,
Still, I ventured in.

I resented taking refuge in the routine it offered.
For fear of the unknown,
I would wish for this unfaltering dream to collapse into
   distant haze.

MIRROR ON THE WALL

In my reflection,
A woman meets my gaze.
Her eyes tell a story of strength.
I had yet to recognize her poise.

ORDINARY

In Haiti, I was not extraordinary.

I would not consider lowering the hood of my jacket on my
    way to the corner store.
Everyone looked like me.

I was not worried about language limiting my tongue.
Everyone spoke like me.

I did not worry about being accepted in surroundings I
    had yet to know.
Everyone loved like me.

In Haiti, I was ordinary.
In Haiti, I was one of many.

It felt like safety.

To be surrounded by a people
Of your kind.
Of your spirit.
Of your mind.

I took comfort in my mundane routine.

Because I was ordinary.

I only began to realize that I was not
When my changed environment told me otherwise.

Before long,

I motioned my eyes side to side as I took every step.
I had to be careful since
Not everyone looked like me.

I was afraid to be too loud, or not be understood.
I had to be careful since
Not everyone spoke like me.

I had to wait before getting too comfortable in a room.
I had to be careful because
Not everyone loved like me.

Now I was on edge.

In rooms bustling with conversation,
I felt out of place.

Extraordinary
— And not in the wonderous way one might assume.
Extraordinary to a fault.

In those moments,

I only wished to be surrounded by a people
Of my kind.
My spirit.
My mind.

LESSONS LEARNED

Too long I have spent trying to claim this world.
This world does not feel my woes.
Or value my prose.
I have learned that.

LANDSCAPES

My horizon shifts.

Concrete roofs and rocky hills turn to
Asphalt shingles and lofty towers.

Yes, this horizon shifts.

Still,
I remain grounded.

FINAL WORDS

Today, the byline reads my name.

It tells my story.
The story of my country.
Of my people.

The story of the ordinary ones.

ACKNOWLEDGEMENTS

Publishing a book was never in my sight. I did not anticipate the amount of work it would take to get here, but I am so glad that I was not alone in this journey. I cannot begin to thank all of the people who have inspired me to this point.

First, I am incredibly grateful for my loving family: Arguio, Chantal, and Arielle. Their support and late-night snacks ultimately gave me the motivation I needed to see the process through.

Including the history and culture of the Haitian people was important for me while writing. I want to thank my father for the hours spent reminiscing on the past, recounting history, and inspiring some of these works. I want to also thank Gabriel Eugene for the research and timeline of this history.

To my amazing beta-readers, Arielle, Laetitia, Mika, Nathan, and Shela, thank you so much for the time you put into this project. Your thoughtful feedback was crucial to the development of these pieces, and I am beyond grateful.

I also want to thank my family, friends, and mentors whose kind words and support encouraged me through the end.

Thank you to everyone on the New Degree Press team who had a hand in making this book possible—development, layout, copyediting, and proofreading. Special thanks to my wonderful editors Elissa and Rebecca who learned with me and guided me throughout this process.

APPENDIX

AUTHOR'S NOTE

Budiman, Abby. "Key Findings about US Immigrants." *Pew Research Center.* August 20, 2020.

www.ingramcontent.com/pod-product-compliance
Lightning Source LLC
LaVergne TN
LVHW011835060526
838200LV00053B/4043